BARE BONES Project Management

What you *can't* **not** do

The book for everyone who has been volunteered to lead a project despite having no training or experience in the discipline

By **Bob Lewis**

Author of *Keep the Joint Running*

✝S SURVIVOR
PUBLISHING

6272 Sequoia Circle
Eden Prairie, Minnesota 55346,
(952) 949-2444

Visit our Web site at **www.issurvivor.com**

BARE BONES **PROJECT MANAGEMENT**

Published by **IS Survivor Publishing,**
6272 Sequoia Circle, Eden Prairie, Minnesota 55346,
(952) 949-2444.

Although the author and publisher have made every effort to ensure the accuracy and completeness of information contained in this book, we assume no responsibility for errors, inaccuracies, omissions or any inconsistency herein. Any slights of people, places or organizations are unintentional.

ISBN 978-0-9749354-2-3
LCCN 2006927011

Design and production by Tim Bitney

DEDICATION

This book is dedicated to the thousands of hardworking professionals who, without ever having received any instruction in the discipline of project management, have ever been told, "We're launching
a project, and you're going to run it."

ACKNOWLEDGEMENTS

My knowledge of professional project management began with formal training and informal coaching from truly superior project managers I worked with while employed as a consultant at Perot Systems. Max Fritzler and Rich Mordhorst in particular deserve credit for broadening and deepening what knowledge I have about the subject.

Pat Fullerton was and still is another outstanding project manager there; it's safe to say I learned more about the discipline from working with her on a project than from any other single source. Pat was kind enough to review the manuscript for this book, which is very much the better for her help.

I also need to thank Dave Kaiser - a very talented CIO, client, and friend - for his perceptive suggestions, and for using the manuscript to help one of his project managers organize a project for his organization. The combination both improved the manuscript and validated its content.

My partner in crime, Steve Nazian, provided his usual, invaluable assistance in improving and refining the contents of the book, and for serving as copy editor. You'd be reading a sloppier piece of work had it not been for his tireless efforts on your behalf.

Somewhere in here I need to thank the Project Management Institute. While I didn't draw directly on its training or Project Management Body of Knowledge (PMBOK), I have no doubt that if you were to trace the material in this book back to its sources, the

PMI would be the most important of them.

And finally, you can thank Tim Bitney for saving you from my amateurish attempts at layout and design. Tim is the one who takes my words and pictures and somehow, magically, transforms them into something that looks like a real book.

To the extent you find this book valuable, these folks deserve a lot of the credit. To the extent you find it irritating or pointless ... it's hard for the author to escape responsibility for that.

CONTENTS

	DEDICATION	iii
	ACKNOWLEDGEMENTS	v
	INTRODUCTION	1
1	SPONSORSHIP AND GOVERNANCE	3
2	UNDERSTAND THE PROJECT	11
3	PROJECT STAFFING - DEFINING "WE"	17
4	PLANNING THE WORK	23
5	THE LAUNCH	33
6	MANAGING THE PROJECT	37
7	DECLARING VICTORY	49

INTRODUCTION

I'm not much of a project manager. Adequate at best. As a top-notch project manager told me once, "You aren't anal-retentive enough to be a good project manager."

Truer words were never spoken. Yet when I do lead projects, they generally finish on time, on budget, and with all deliverables intact. What's my secret?

That's what this book is about: How to manage projects when you aren't a professional project manager, don't plan on becoming a professional project manager, and mostly hope to survive the experience so you can get back to your chosen career.

But can fifty-two pages provide enough information to get you through? Sure. Not enough to help you build a nuclear submarine or office building. But for small projects, these techniques work.

This book started as a consulting engagement. A new client was having problems with its project management.

Okay, problems is an understatement. "Project completion" had become an oxymoron, to the point that a nine-month project was in its third year, with no end in sight. As I poked into the project, what had gone wrong, and the company's habits in undertaking projects, I found that the problems weren't due to the lack of a sophisticated project management methodology. The changes I recommended were, in fact, simple:

> Break up large, monolithic projects into roadmaps of small ones. (The techniques for building this kind of roadmap are

beyond the scope of this book. It's still good advice. If you find yourself in charge of a project that will last longer than nine months, with a core project team of more than a dozen, break it up into smaller, more manageable chunks.)

> Insist on every project having a business sponsor (Chapter 1).
> Give every project a clean start (Chapters 2 and 5).
> Make sure every project is allowed to end (Chapter 7).

The client agreed to give them a try. Two years later, on a return visit, project completion had become routine.

Since that time I've advised several other clients that have found project completion to be a challenge. None of them required complex solutions. Mostly, they required ... well, they required what you'll find in the next fifty-two pages.

I hope you appreciate them, because if you read and follow the advice they contain, that will be one less reason to engage the services of my consulting company.

I'm slitting my own throat.

SPONSORSHIP AND GOVERNANCE

Let's define "project" (otherwise we could spend the rest of this book at cross purposes). A project is a collection of tasks, involving multiple individuals, organized to deliver well-defined products (called "deliverables" in project parlance) within a defined period of time.

Before you manage a project ... before you even consider managing a project, let alone start planning the tasks, selecting the team or anything else ... make sure it has a chance of succeeding. That means being able to answer four questions:

1. What, when all is said and done, is the point of the project?
2. Who in authority wants it to succeed?
3. Who has the authority to define success?
4. Who has the authority to make different kinds of decisions and resolve different kinds of issues, and to delegate that authority when the situation calls for it?

WHAT'S THE POINT?

We've defined "project." Now let's define "business projects where there's a point to undertaking them." The point of any business project is to deliver business improvement of some kind - a different, better way of doing things. Expending time, effort and budget so everything stays exactly the same as it was before wastes the time, effort and budget.

Businesses can improve in just three ways - they can increase revenue, reduce cost, or mitigate risk. Everything else is technique. Many of the other, commonly stated project outcomes are valid, of course. That's because they contribute to one or more of the big three. For example, the improvement of employee morale is a perfectly fine project goal, but only because improved employee morale usually results in harder work and better attention to results, which in turn improves all three of the big three.

Similar arguments can be made for many other commonly used project rationales, such as improved customer satisfaction, quality, cycle time and so on. In the end, it's a business project, which means it should lead to business improvement, which means that in some way, shape or form the business should take in more money, spend less money, or be at less risk than before the project started.

WHO CARES?

Just because the business improves doesn't mean it improves for anyone working there; almost certainly it won't improve for everyone working there. And in particular, it doesn't mean all of the company's top executives will like the result. In the executive suite, most business change results in winners and losers.

That's okay. You don't need everyone to want the result. You do, however, need to make sure that someone does. It isn't automatic, because of how most projects come about.

Here's how it usually happens:

1. Someone somewhere has a bright idea …
2. Refines it until the description sounds worthwhile …
3. And pushes the resulting "business case" into the company's project approval process.
4. The approval process assesses whether the business case properly and credibly describes costs, benefits, relationship to business strategy and so on …
5. And delivers a decision as to whether it's approved or not.

Deciding a project is worthwhile isn't the same as chartering a project that can succeed. To succeed, someone with the authority to make decisions - to provide more time, resources and budget - has to be committed[1] to it.

Distinguishing between the individual who had the bright idea and an executive who wants it badly enough to commit to it is criti-

---

[1] As an old and worthwhile wisecrack has it, the difference between involvement and commitment is that when you have steak and eggs the hen was involved but the cow was committed.

cal to your personal future. That's because there are lots of great ideas, but a huge shortage of executives willing to commit to the value of a proposed business improvement. The name for an executive willing to do so is "business sponsor," and without one you won't be leading a viable project. (The usual term used to label the person who had the bright idea and sold it to the company, if you're interested, is "champion.")

What should happen is that every project has a sponsor before it's assigned a project manager. What usually does happen is that the champion, project manager and chief information officer list likely sponsors and then try to recruit one.

And what happens far too often is that if they fail to do so, they list the CIO as sponsor and move forward at flank speed toward near-certain disaster.

You can run a project without a business sponsor. The odds you'll complete it are much worse, though, because it's the business sponsor who has the authority to add time, budget and resources, and ensure they actually show up when they're needed. These are eventualities that frequently come up during the course of a project. They do for any number of reasons, only some of which are related to how well you manage it.

Even more significant is this: Without a business sponsor you can't achieve the point of it all. That's because most business changes inflict pain - at least in the short term - on someone. Having someone with the authority to say, "We're going to do it anyway," is the difference between avoiding the pain by resisting the change and doing it anyway.

DEFINING SUCCESS

Among the more common experiences project managers go through on a regular basis [2] is an argument as to whether the project is finished. "We've completed every deliverable," the project manager explains.

"But you haven't given me anything I can use," the sponsor, champion, or other stakeholder responds.

"Every deliverable meets or exceeds specifications," the project manager answers, starting to lose patience.

"I don't care about the specifications. It's useless."

"If the specs were wrong you should have said so before we

---

[2] "Regular basis" is defined as at least once per project completion.

used them to build the software!"

"As far as I'm concerned, the specs were a bunch of gibberish! You guys told me the project couldn't start until I signed off on them, so I signed off on them!"

And so on.

▼ ▼

CRITICAL SUCCESS FACTOR:
BUSINESS CHANGE MANAGEMENT
While beyond the scope of this book, Business Change Management - the discipline of anticipating and dealing with resistance to the planned business change - is a very important subject for project managers.

Business change management covers six major subject areas:
> *Stakeholder analysis - who might support or resist the change, and for what reasons.*
> *Involvement plan - who will do what work and be assigned authority to make which decisions.*
> *Metrics plan - by what criteria will the business decide whether the project has achieved its purpose ... the point.*
> *Training plan - how will business users be taught how to do their work the new way that the project is supposed to support.*
> *Culture change plan - many business changes require a different way for employees to assess situations and respond to them.*
> *Communication plan - communication includes organizational listening, informing, and persuading. All three are required to successfully anticipate, discover, and address resistance to business change.*
Included in the discipline is designing the change and implementation strategy so as to minimize the extent to which the change inflicts short-term pain, minimizing even more the extent to which the change is purely harmful to some groups, and building tasks into the project plan for dealing with the kinds of resistance most likely to arise.

Many organizations try to prevent this dysfunction by improving the methodologies they use to define specifications. They get better and better at fixing what isn't the root cause of the problem.

The root cause is, nobody knows who has the authority to define success [3] - to look at the project's results, declare them to be good, and allow everyone to go back to their normal jobs or on to the next project. The only alternative is for the project manager to try to make every stakeholder happy, which isn't possible because the only way to make Stakeholder A happy is to make changes which

[3] Credit where it's due: I first encountered this very practical insight in an article by Ed Yourdan.

will make Stakeholder B unhappy and vice versa.

There are only two ways to address this situation effectively. The better [4] of the two is that it's the project sponsor. The second, viable answer is to form a steering committee composed of representatives of all stakeholder groups ... and this is very important: representatives who have the authority to make decisions during Steering Committee meetings ... and have it meet to review the deliverables and either declare them good or agree among themselves what will be required to make them good.

MAKING DECISIONS

First, a reminder: A decision commits (or denies) time, budget or resources. Everything else is just talking about it.

Which brings up a vital issue in every project: Who gets to make decisions? The increasingly popular term "governance" is the fifty-buck synonym for establishing a clear, shared understanding of who has the authority to make different kinds of project decisions. Without effective governance, projects can grind to a halt while waiting for a simple but potentially risky decision. To provide just one example among zillions: You're managing a software development project. As you get close to the finish line it becomes clear that the production software will require a bigger and more expensive server than the initial specifications called for. This will add $150,000 to the original project budget.

Who gets to say yes?

In the best of all possible situations (and we've already defined "best") there are only two answers - the project manager and the project sponsor, and the two have a clear agreement regarding which the former must escalate to the latter.

In the second-best situation, there are three answers - the project manager, project sponsor, and steering committee, which meets both monthly and as needed to resolve issues - with clear criteria regarding which issues each can resolve.

The third-best situation starts to get messy. It adds an "Advisory Committee" of some sort composed of stakeholders who have limited political clout but useful insights regarding design details.

Then there's the worst [5] of all possible situations: Those who ought to define governance, unwilling to establish clarity in

---

[4] "Best" is defined as "makes the situation most convenient for the project manager."

[5] "Worst" is defined as what always happens unless you take active steps to prevent it.

advance, instead tell you they'll deal with issues on a case-by-case basis. Which is the opposite of governance. So don't allow it. Speak these simple words: "I can't, because I won't know which issues I can resolve and which we have to deal with on a case-by-case basis."

"If you're the right person for the job," you'll be told, "you'll have good judgment about this."

"I do have good judgment about this," you answer. "That doesn't mean it will always match everyone else's good judgment. I'm just suggesting we all pool our good judgment once, now, instead of over-and-over again."

THE SHORT VERSION

When you manage a project, your best-case scenario is to have just one individual in the business to whom you're accountable - the project sponsor. The sponsor has the authority to make all decisions, resolve all issues, decide when the project has succeeded, and most important of all, has the drive and desire, deep in the gut, to want the project to succeed in the first place.

You won't always get the best-case scenario. You can, however, insist that you have clear project governance. You can insist on it because as project manager you're being completely reasonable asking who will resolve issues and make decisions that exceed your authority.

You can't insist on sponsorship, although you should do the best you can. One reason is a political nicety corporations would prefer you didn't notice: A too-large number of business projects [6], and especially IT projects [7], are orphans. Many business executives want them, but no business executive wants them enough to take any risks on their behalf.

The usual root cause is that the project is good for the company without being good for any of its executives. Conversely, many project proposals are highly desirable for one or two executives without having any real potential for increasing revenue, reducing cost, or mitigating risk. Unsurprisingly, you'll find it easier to find sponsors for projects that are good for an executive's career without improving the company than for projects that help the company

[6] "Too large" is defined as any number larger than zero.

[7] Different subject for a different book: There is no such thing as an IT project in the first place, although there are projects led by IT project managers and plenty of business projects that require the delivery of information technology.

without creating a career advantage for any of its senior executives. Given a choice, having a sponsor is better than having a point. Not much better, but better.

Still, if you can't establish sponsorship, governance, and a valid point to it all, do what King Arthur and company did in response to French taunting in *Monty Python and the Holy Grail*: Run away! Because without all three, as project manager you'll be left holding the bag at the end. After all, you were managing the project, it didn't result in success, and as everyone knows it's important to Hold People Accountable [8].

STEP BY STEP
For your project to have a chance of success:

1. It has to have a point (a business outcome that warrants the investment in time, staff and budget).
2. At least one business executive has to personally want it enough to take risks on its behalf …
3. … And has the authority to commit time, budget and staff if they're needed.
4. … And has the authority and willingness to decide when it's finished.
5. All stakeholders have to agree about project governance - about who has the authority to make different decisions about the project.

---

[8] "Hold People Accountable" is, of course, ManagementSpeak for "find a convenient scapegoat."

UNDERSTAND THE PROJECT

Lots of factors can cause projects to fail. One of the most common is that the members of a project team are each working on a different project, or at least they aren't working on the exact same project.

A psychologist named Tuckman explained the problem in the antediluvian year 1965. Teams, Tuckman explained, start out with the unstable combination of a high degree of trust and a low degree of alignment. Members are, in other words, enthusiastic about the journey that lies in front of them, confident their teammates are just as enthusiastic about the journey, and about to embark on as many different journeys as there are members of the team.

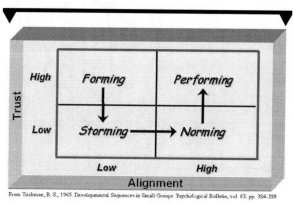

From Tuckman, B. S., 1965. Developmental Sequences in Small Groups. Psychological Bulletin, vol. 63. pp. 384-399

Figure 1/ *The stages of team formation*

They just don't know it yet. But when they find out, it gets ugly fast. When the members of a project team discover their apparently strong initial consensus wasn't consensus at all, each member feels betrayed by the others. It's a frustrating experience. Inside each team member's head is a thought similar to this: "Everyone had agreed on this point. Now you've changed your mind, which means we have to start all over!" Sometimes, two team members think this about each other, regarding the same point, at the same moment.

When a project reaches this stage, tempers often flare, even among mature, experienced professionals. The root cause is pretty simple: The English language is imprecise under the best of circumstances, and is made even less precise by the linguistic laziness of many of its practitioners.

So the agreements team members thought they'd made were, in fact, misunderstandings. They were using the same words to mean different things, different words to mean the same thing, and "thing" to mean just about everything.

That's what happened. The conclusion each member of the team reaches is, "It's your fault! I can't trust you anymore!" And the team dissolves into heated arguments - "storming" to use Tuckman's vocabulary - the stage at which both alignment and trust are at their lowest.

The good news about heated arguments is that nobody holds back in the interest of diplomacy. With decent leadership and facilitation team members sort out the misunderstandings, agree to shared definitions of terms, and find ways to compromise when they clarify where they truly disagree. They line up their thinking and are finally, if not on the same page, at least reading from the same script. They don't trust each other again ... not yet ... but at least they're aligned. Tuckman calls this "norming."

With alignment, and a few weeks without major blow-ups, team members can rebuild their trust based on actual agreement instead of illusions. When this happens the team enters the "performing" stage and productive work can begin.

What can you, as project manager, do to prevent this waste of time and effort?

Nothing. You can't. It's in the nature of things, built into the fabric of time, space, and human communication.

What you can do is get through it quicker, and with less damage. It's a two stage process.

The first stage is to carefully define the project. That's the purpose of a document called a "Statement of Work" or SOW (pronounced "ess oh double-u," not "Sow"). There's value in preparing the actual document, even though it's unlikely anyone will read it, as doing so helps you rehearse your explanations. If you don't, at least make sure you can readily explain the five most important subjects SOWs typically cover. They are the project's objective, context, goals, deliverables, and scope. Here they are, in sequence, to describe a typical software project.

OBJECTIVE

The objective is the point of it all - what the business is trying to accomplish. A statement of objectives should include the point of it all (see Chapter 1), overall timeframe, a quick statement of what it means to be complete, and another of what it means to be successful. For example:

The objective of this project is to build the software tools necessary for dramatic improvements in the throughput, cycle time, and cost of operating our distribution warehouse. The project will be considered complete when, in approximately six months, the software has been completed, tested, and demonstrated to comply with the specifications. It will be considered successful when the software is in productive use and the distribution warehouse has achieved its performance goals.

That's it. Short, sweet, succinct - a summary of what the project team is supposed to deliver, coupled with an equally brief synopsis of what the business will gain from it. Nobody will have the patience for anything longer anyway, and besides, we're explaining what the point is ... and points aren't big and bulky.

Speaking of points, here's one, and as project manager you need to embrace it: The objective - the business objective - isn't delivery of working software. That's a means to an end, which is why the objective statement differentiates between project completion and project success. The confusion of means and ends is one of the primary reasons some projects complete on schedule, only to be followed by months of post-completion fix-ups.

CONTEXT

When you're explaining a project, the point isn't enough. The reason the point is worth pursuing also matters. That's what the context is for - to ... well, to put the project in context. Hence the name.

When ABCCo built its warehouse, the company's sole means of sales was through its large network of small stores. The warehouse's internal processes, and the information technology built to support them, were all geared to support a logistics model in which small, frequent shipments were the norm.

Since that time the company has added a "big box" store cate-gory, which has proven more successful than the original small/mall model. It has also added catalog and e-commerce sales channels. Big box stores require a different distribution pattern than small stores. Catalog and e-commerce require fulfillment - "pick, pack and ship" - processes. Neither the warehouse, its processes, nor its software were designed to support any of these changes, and the result has been an accumulation of short-term patches sufficient to continue operating, but not to operate efficiently.

This project is part of a larger initiative that includes process re-engineering and other restructurings needed to address these limita-tions.

The context explains, in general terms, why the project is worth undertaking, how it fits into a larger undertaking if that is the case, and why the objective is worth achieving. Making it clear helps project team members understand what's expected of them in the same way. Just as important, by providing the context you create an environment in which each project team member can look for additional opportunities, discover holes in the specifications, and resolve any ambiguities they encounter.

GOALS

Goals describe the specific outcomes that should result from the project. Where the *Objective* is a general explanation of the point of it all, Goals are more precise. If it's a purchasing project, the goals might be to reduce the cost of raw materials while ensuring everything needed for the production schedule arrives at the factory at least four hours and no more than two days before needed.

For the example we've been using:

The goals of this project are to:

> *Provide the business with the software it needs to support its new warehouse processes.*
> *Create a software work product that minimizes the cost of maintenance over its useful life.*
> *Provide other teams within the larger warehouse re-engi-neering initiative - such as the training team - with the infor-mation they need to succeed in achieving their objectives.*

Goals are what the project is to achieve - its contribution to the planned business changes which, when implemented, will result in the intended business benefit.

DELIVERABLES

Deliverables are products - the tangible outputs of a project that everyone inside and outside the team can point to, look at, inspect, and admire (or, more likely in a software project, gripe about and nitpick to death). They're what you deliver - hence the name.

This project will produce these deliverables:

> *Software specifications based on the warehouse processes being designed by the Warehouse Redesign Project (interim deliverable).*

> *A software test plan that includes unit, integration, regression, end-user acceptance, and stress testing.*

> *Software applications built to these specifications, and tested according to the test plan, suitable for use in the warehouse processes being designed by the Warehouse Redesign Project.*

> *Technical and end-user documentation for the software.*

Deliverables and goals can overlap, but they aren't the same thing, any more than selling a car is the same thing as providing reliable transportation. The distinctions among objectives, goals and deliverables might seem like unimportant semantics. They aren't. The project's purpose, outcomes, and tangible work products are very different subjects. The project team should understand all three. The first explains importance, the second explains utility, and the third tells everyone how they'll know when the project is finished so they can declare victory, relax, and have a beer.

SCOPE

A project's scope is a statement of what is included, as opposed to what isn't included - what's out of scope. Strictly speaking, what's in scope is what's required to create the specified Deliverables (above) - nothing more, nothing less. As such, no scope statement should be required, nor would it be required if it weren't for Tuckman.

In the projects you're likely to manage, though, participants and stakeholders sometimes misunderstand each other. You'd like to minimize the extent to which that happens. The scope section of the SOW is your opportunity ... not to restate the deliverables, but to cover any likely misaligned expectations. If your project's deliverable is software, you might explain that designing the software, writing specifications, coding, and testing are in scope but training end-users and making sure the software is used properly are not. In our example:

This project is limited to software development and testing. Resolution of design inconsistencies is within its scope, but changes to the associated business process designs are the responsibility of other projects and therefore out of scope.

The same is true of the tasks required for software deployment, staff training, and institution of the new processes the software has been designed to support.

TO SUM UP

Under the best of circumstances, people misunderstand each other. Project teams, under pressure to deliver results on tight deadlines and unaccustomed to working together, are more susceptible than most, especially during the early stages. It's your job to minimize this. Before you can, your own understanding of the project has to be clear.

That's the point of this section: Limiting the damage that can come from misaligned expectations, and in particular avoiding the I-thought-you-were-going-to-do-that syndrome.

STEP BY STEP

Members of project teams don't start out with the same understanding of the project they're about to work on, resulting in a loss of trust and effectiveness, until they work through their misunderstandings and conflicting thoughts and assumptions.

It's up to you as project manager to minimize the extent to which this happens. To do so you first need a clear understanding of the project yourself. To achieve this clarity you have to understand the project's:

1. Objective - the point of it all.
2. Context - why it makes sense, and what other undertakings it's connected to.
3. Goals - what specific business improvements are supposed to occur.
4. Deliverables - the specific work products the project team is supposed to create.
5. Scope - a clear understanding of the project's boundaries: What's in and what's out.

PROJECT STAFFING - DEFINING "WE"

The world, according to most members of most project teams, is divided into "we" and "they." We are the source of all that's good in the world. We toil in anonymity, unappreciated by the beneficiaries of our long hours and hard work.

They put barriers in our path, fail to provide any help, break their promises, make unreasonable demands, and generally aggravate the snot out of us.

As project manager there's not very much you can do about this attitude, other than exploit it. It's in the nature of teams. Anyone who isn't part of the team isn't trustworthy the way someone who's on the team is. After all, they haven't gone through the process of forming, storming, and norming (see previous chapter). They just don't understand.

One of the secrets of successful project management is making sure everyone required for project success is part of "we." The only alternative is for them to be "they." Here's the difference: People who are "we" collaborate to achieve success. People who are "they" criticize, without understanding enough of the specifics to do so usefully.

Another of the secrets of successful project management is making sure all tasks are included in the project plan, and the staff needed to perform the tasks are part of the project team. This might seem like an obvious requirement, but in practice it's easy to miss a few pieces. For example:

> Will your project require some new hardware - a server or two? Make sure someone from systems administration is listed as a team member.
> How about network traffic? Is it possible your project will have enough of an impact to delay the roll-out? Include a network engineer.
> Is a software vendor involved? Somewhere in the vendor's employ is a technician who wants to be part of this effort. He or she doesn't realize it just yet. It's up to you to make it happen.
> Then there's the Facilities department. Many projects require redesign and build-out of one or more workspaces.

The alternative to making these people part of the team is to go begging to them, hat in hand, when the time comes for them to deliver their contributions to the project. If they're on the team, their work is defined by communicated and agreed-upon tasks and deadlines. If they aren't on the team, their work is defined by requests for which they might or might not have a defined service level. That means you have to get in line, behind everyone else who also has a request that's just as urgent to them as yours is to you.

While it's often done wrong, this point reflects a very basic principle of management theory: As project manager, you're responsible for the project schedule. Unless the people needed to execute every project task are part of the project team, you lack the authority that's supposed to be commensurate with your responsibility.

Your project is a big pile of work. You need to make sure you have enough hands (and the right hands) to hold the shovels needed to remove it - one goal of project staffing. The other is making sure your authority and responsibility match.

Project staff fall into two groups. The first is the core team - those members needed to do the leading and heavy lifting, and who spend at least half their time working on project tasks. The second is the extended team, composed of everyone else who also needs to be "we," those who have just one or two tasks to perform, and those you need to participate as "subject matter experts," (SMEs, in ConsultantSpeak).

The core team is relatively easy to figure out. List the kinds of tasks the project will require every day. In a software development effort, that means developers and maybe a software architect. Depending on your methodology, you'll also need a business analyst or two, and perhaps a business manager and one or two end-users.

That leaves the extended team. Start by listing the types of expertise core team members might need to draw on from time to time, and those bits and pieces of work the core team can't take on. For software development, that might mean a data analyst, software quality assurance analyst, user-interface specialist, and a trainer, along with the aforementioned system administrator and network engineer.

Then figure out who, if they aren't with you, are likely to be against you. That list includes, but certainly isn't limited to compliance or internal audit, corporate communications, information security, various managers of various departments likely to be affected by the project in one way or another, and, most important of all, several end-user representatives - if, that is, none are part of the core team.

Why do you want to clutter up your project with so many people who won't be performing project tasks? An example illustrates: If you include compliance and information security, you can design a secure, auditable system instead of having to retrofit after development is done. It's the difference between a game of pin-the-tail-on-the-donkey, where you try to hit the target while blindfolded, and having, not just open eyes, but guides to help you navigate.

All those other folks in the middle? You have only two choices: Turn them into critics, or into collaborators. If they're collaborators they'll find reasons to like what you're building. If they aren't, they'll do their best to be helpful by putting your work under a microscope to help you find flaws. As one CIO put it, regarding a complainer against the project whom he added to the team, "I would rather have him inside the tent spitting out than outside the tent spitting in on us."[9]

How about those pesky end-users? Isn't it quicker and more fun to develop the system without them, so at the end you can surprise them with the gift of new software?

Well, no. Many methodologies include a formal testing step called End-User Acceptance Testing. All too often it's also called Make Major Changes for No Apparent Reason. End-User Acceptance Testing should take place all the time. Jill the developer should feel comfortable picking up the phone, dialing an extension that's been called so often the numbers have worn off her telephone keypad,

---

[9] He was paraphrasing Lyndon Johnson, who used a word different from "spitting."

and saying, "Hey, Jack, when you have a minute can you drop by? I've made a few changes to the order entry screen and I'd like your reaction to them."

A software project is a pretty big hill. It's better if … yes, that's right … Jack and Jill climb the hill together. Regular end-user input keeps projects from going off-course, and provides a strong sense of ownership in the result.

As project manager, it's a good idea to formally document who you're going to need on the project and how much you'll need them. When in doubt, use a table - unless you're a consultant, of course, at which point you should use a matrix[10] instead. Table 1 shows a typical Staffing Plan (or, if you're a consultant, refer to Matrix 1 instead).

Note that the staffing plan doesn't necessarily name the members of the project team, or even how many people you'll need in each role[11]. If you have enough information to do so, by all means

Table 1/ Sample Staffing Plan

Role	Source	Responsibilities	Commitment
Project Manager	IT Application Support	Project leadership, administration and structure.	100%
Developers	IT Application Support	Design, code and unit test application code.	100%
Database Analyst/ Data Designer	Information Resources Management	Provide advice, consulting and final review of database schema changes.	10%
SQA Analyst	Software Quality Assurance Team	Develop test plan and test scripts; perform integration, regression and stress tests.	20%
Subject Matter Experts	Affected business areas	Provide information and documentation as needed for project success.	5%
Business Sponsor	John Smith	Provides guidance to project managers/teams on direction, resolves issues beyond the authority of the project team and IT sponsor, and in general oversees the initiative to ensure proper business perspectives are incorporated into plans, designs, and deliverables.	2 hrs/wk

Matrix 1/ Sample Staffing Plan

[10] The difference? A table has columns and rows. A matrix, in contrast, has rows and columns, and sounds much more technical.

[11] Somewhere between the "understanding the project" activities described in Chapter 2 and the staffing plan described here, someone will ask for an estimate of the project's cost. The answer lies in a black art called "Project Estimation," which is outside the scope of this book. Developing a project budget is within its scope - you'll find the technique in Chapter 4.

Decision	Core team	Data analyst	System admin	Order entry end-users	Accting end-users	Customer service	Date due	Date done	Decision
System architecture	R	C	C				2/5/06	2/5/06	See architecture spec
Data design	R	A,C					2/19/06	2/18/06	See ERD and schemas
Server sizing	C	C	R				4/3/06		
Screen layouts	R			C	C	C	Project plan		
Report layouts	C	C		R	R	R	Project plan		
Office furniture	I			R	R	R	3/15/06		

Table 2/ Sample RACI Chart (Responsible/Accountable/Consulted/Informed)

do. If you don't, it isn't a reason to figure out what roles the project will need covered.

TURNING "THEY" INTO "WE"

Before leaving the subject of project staffing, there's one more subject worth covering: How to turn a they into a we. The answer is to give them something important to decide. A handy tool for keeping track is the "RACI Chart," RACI standing for "Responsible, Accountable, Consulted, Informed" (Table 2).

The idea is to make sure every important constituency owns at least one important decision in the project, and is involved in as many of the other decisions affecting them as is practical. It's a simple idea that pays two dividends. First, it gets the project team off the hook. If, for example, end-users will be moving into new cubicles, let them design the new cubicles, or at least be part of the design effort. That way, if anyone doesn't like the result, they probably won't say anything anyway because it will have been their co-workers who made the decision, and they'll be right there, sitting in one of them, if anyone wants to know why that particular design was chosen.

And second, it lets the project team focus on core project tasks. Some decisions aren't critical to the project's major deliverables but are nonetheless time-consuming to make - especially if due diligence is required, or if they must be made by consensus. These are usually best left to those who will have to live with them.

Tip: Some end-user participants figure their role in the project confers an enhanced status that means they speak for all end-users rather than representing them. Emphasize the need for them to talk with their co-workers instead of imposing their own judgment.

One other note: Take a look at the data design. In this example, the data analyst is both accountable for the design, and consulted, but it's the project team that's responsible for doing the actual work. This is a perfectly reasonable way to involve the data analyst group, although of course it isn't the only way: Using a different methodology, the data analyst could have been made responsible, consulting the core team as part of the design process.

That's about it. A basic rule of project management is that if a project requires that a task be done or a decision made, those who have to perform the task or make the decision must be part of the project team.

If they aren't, there's no reasonable way the project manager can take responsibility for finishing the project on time. Not a bad thing if you're looking for an excuse, of course. If, instead, you want to get the job done, this is one of the most critical steps in making sure you can.

STEP BY STEP

Staff projects with a core team and an extended team. Core team members:

1. *Perform the heavy lifting.*
2. *Are committed at least 50% to project tasks.*

Extended team members:

1. *Are committed to the project less than 50% of their average work week.*
2. *Provide special expertise to the core team.*
3. *Perform "bits-and-pieces" tasks core team members are either unequipped or unauthorized for.*
4. *Are better as "we" than as "they."*

PLANNING THE WORK

In the beginning, according to the Judeo-Christian Bible, was the Word. Considering the author it was most probably a top-notch Word, more than good enough to serve as the Objective. To describe a whole universe, though, one Word probably wasn't enough. My guess: God didn't just keep typing. He used an outline.

No matter what your job, no matter what you're trying to think through, you need to be good at outlining. It's the definitive, time-tested way to turn a vague notion into a clear, precise, detailed explanation.

Project management is no exception to this rule. Good project managers are good outliners, because outlining is how a project manager turns an objective into a plan. Except that because "outline" sounds like something you do in high school English class, project managers call their outlines "Work Breakdown Structures" - WBS is the accepted acronym. Use it and be cool.

Also, use project management software. It won't make you particularly cool, nor will it turn you into a great project manager. What it will do is make the mechanics of creating (and updating) a WBS and project timeline a lot easier.

CREATING A WORK BREAKDOWN STRUCTURE

Most of the secret of successful project planning is little more than outlining. To understand why, start listing all of the specific tasks project team members will have to complete for the project to finish

▼

WAREHOUSE MANAGEMENT SYSTEM PROJECT

> Launch project
> Gather data
> Develop specifications
> Write software
> Test software
> Shut down project

Figure 2/ First-level project tasks

▼

WAREHOUSE MANAGEMENT SYSTEM PROJECT

> Launch project
> Gather information requirements
>   o   Conduct interviews
>   o   Observe work processes
>   o   Determine information
>   domains
>   o   Develop information model
> Develop specifications
> Write software
> Test software
> Shut down project

Figure 3/ Second-level project tasks

successfully as they occur to you. See? You can't make sense of it.

Now, instead, make a list of the major chunks of work required. You should get a list something like Figure 2. Didn't take much thought, did it? That's what you want - to not have to think very hard. It isn't that hard thinking is a bad thing, exactly. It's that hard thinking leads to complicated results, and complicated results mean you're never entirely sure you got it right.

Next, drill down a level for each of the high-level project tasks. For example, "Gather Data" might end up looking like Figure 3. Still not too complicated. It still isn't supposed to be.

Drill down another level. The work is starting to come into focus. That's all there is to it when it comes to developing a WBS - keep adding levels until further refinement is pointless - until you've gone beyond "put on socks and shoes," to start explaining how to put on socks. The other way you know you're done is that you won't have much trouble estimating how much time each task will require for completion.

You aren't quite done, though. A good habit is to make sure each major group of tasks finishes with a milestone - an event tied to delivery of a tangible work product. The value of a milestone is that it establishes recognizable progress. Until then, progress is, to a certain extent, a matter of opinion. Once you've reached a milestone there's no doubt. Figure 4 shows this next level of task refinement, finishing with a milestone.

One advantage to using project management software instead of an electronic spreadsheet is that the former makes the outlining process simple. Every package you're likely to encounter lets you define tasks, sub-tasks, sub-sub-tasks and so on with just a click or two. Spreadsheets don't do that. Don't work any harder than you have to.

Project management software makes the mechanics of outlining simple. Only one thing can make creation of the outline itself simple, and that's starting with a pre-existing outline, developed for a similar project that ended up as a success. Without one you're in for some hard work.

THE PROJECT TIMELINE

Once you've developed the WBS, the rest is easy. Well, relatively easy. You've already broken the project down into tasks that are short and straightforward enough to let you make reasonably accurate guesses about how long they'll take. Now it's time to make those guesses. If you've stopped at the right level of detail in your WBS, most tasks will require between one and two weeks .

▼   ▼

WAREHOUSE MANAGEMENT SYSTEM PROJECT

> *Launch project*
> *Gather information requirements*
>> o *Conduct interviews*
>>> - *List interview sources*
>>> - *Develop interview questions*
>>> - *Schedule interviews*
>>> - *Perform and document interviews*
>>> - *Interpret interviews*
>>> - *Milestone: Publish interview documentation*
>> o *Observe work processes*
>> o *Determine information domains*
>> o *Develop information model*
> *Develop specifications*
> *Write software*
> *Test software*
> *Shut down project*

Figure 4/ Third-level project tasks

Which gets to two risks you'll face when developing a WBS. If you're a "big-picture thinker," you're at risk of insufficient detail. If some tasks require more than two weeks, you need a finer breakdown. With insufficient detail your project can become seriously off-track without your having any way to know it. The result: Significant unplanned delays in project delivery.

If, on the other hand, you're a diligent, hard-working, careful thinker - one who goes beyond "put on socks and shoes" to "locate socks, locate shoes, put on left sock, then right sock, then left shoe, then right shoe, then tie left shoe, and finally tie right shoe," you're also going to be responsible for major project delays. They'll be planned delays, but they'll be delays all the same. Here's why:

When tasks are too granular, you'll probably overestimate each of them. Moving beyond the footware example, it's very likely that you'll use an hour or a day as your minimum standard unit of time. So if you break down a one week task into 14 sub-tasks, you're likely to assign a standard one-day duration to each of them, turning one week of effort into two weeks of effort.

Again: As a general guideline, a good WBS breaks work down to tasks that will require one to two weeks to complete.

Two other bits and pieces about the timeline: First, here's another advantage from using project management software instead of a spreadsheet: It makes entering task durations easy[12].

And second, you don't estimate milestones. A milestone, by definition, happens in no time. It gets a duration of zero.

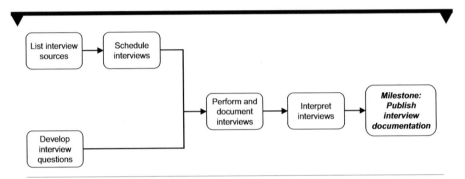

Figure 5/ *Task dependencies*

TASK DEPENDENCIES

In a typical project, some tasks can happen in parallel - for example, different project team members can talk with different interviewees at the same time - while others have to happen in a logical sequence. When one task can't begin until another ends, you have a "dependency." More precisely, you have a "finish-to-start" dependency. The need to define task dependencies is another reason to use project management software instead of a spreadsheet - project management software is designed to keep track of dependencies and use them to automatically calculate when each task should start and finish.

Trick o' the trade: One of the reasons to finish groups of tasks with milestones is that doing so makes the process of managing dependencies simpler when revising a project plan. If you discover you forgot an important task and have to insert it in the middle of a sequence, you're less likely to have to redefine a lot of dependencies throughout the plan if most are attached to milestones instead of tasks in the middle of a sequence.

In the Warehouse Management System Project WBS we've

---

[12] Project management software also makes it easy to handle holidays. You simply define non-work days to the system and it takes that into account when it computes the schedule.

been developing, *List interview sources* and *Develop interview questions* are independent. *Schedule interviews* is dependent on *List interview sources* for obvious reasons. *Perform interviews* is dependent on *Develop interview questions* and *Schedule interviews*. And so on. Figure 5 illustrates task interdependencies for the interviewing process.

ASSIGNING STAFF

Until you know who's going to do what, you don't have a plan. You need to put names on tasks.

It's right about here that project planning becomes tricky. If you assign the same individual to two tasks that aren't dependent - say, to both *List interview sources* and *Develop interview questions*, the tasks become dependent, because unless it's Leonardo Da Vinci, your team member won't be able to *List interview sources* on one sheet of paper with his left hand while he simultaneously *Develops interview questions* on a different sheet of paper with his right hand.

The formal term for this kind of task interdependency is "resource conflict." Theoretically, project management software can take care of the details for you - most packages give you the option of automatically adjusting the timeline so that team members only have to work on one task at a time.

That's the theory. It works well in practice for full-time team members assigned to tasks they can work on full time from start to finish.

Some tasks don't work that way. Take, for example, *Perform and document interviews*. Unless whoever is assigned to *Schedule interviews* achieves perfection, the interview schedule will include gaps. During those gaps, the team members who interview and document when interviewees are available can work on other project tasks.

Project management software handles intermittent tasks like this rather badly.

Also handled badly: Project team members whose participation is intermittent. A steady partial commitment is fine. If a team member has a 50% commitment to the project, meaning 20 hours per week, and you assign her to a one week task, the software will automatically stretch the task to two calendar weeks. If, on the other hand, the 50% commitment means 50% over the life of the project -some weeks full time, others spent doing something else entirely

- the software will just get in the way.

It also gets in the way when some project team members are interchangeable for some tasks. Imagine, for example, three equally competent developers are working on a project that will require their programming 73 software objects. What you'd like to do is tell the software, "Assign programmers to these modules so as to create the most efficient schedule."

It's entirely possible someone has developed project management software that lets you do exactly that. If so, your loyal author has no idea which one it is.

Trick o' the trade: Until you fully master the idiosyncrasies of your project management software, you're probably best off using a user-definable field to contain assignee names, and otherwise applying brute-force workarounds, instead of trying to get the software's highly sophisticated "resource management" features to create a practical project schedule.

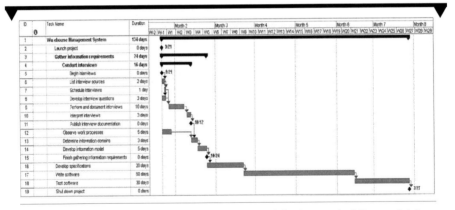

Figure 6/ *Gantt chart for Warehouse Management System project (incomplete)*

GANTT CHARTS

The standard way of representing a project timeline is called a "Gantt chart." These were developed as a production control tool in 1917 by Henry L. Gantt, an American engineer and social scientist, and who was, undoubtedly, a fine project manager. His eponymous charts, however (Figure 6), are pretty much useless for managing projects.

This doesn't make them useless, though. Gantt charts are valuable for communicating project timelines to business sponsors and other management stakeholders, for the simple reason that they show the timetable, dependencies and bottlenecks at a glance.

For actually managing the project, on the other hand, you need a different representation. Best is a simple report that shows who is supposed to work on what, and when (Figure 7). It's what you, and more importantly, project team members need to know. Fortunately, it's pretty easy to get your project management software to print both views depending on what you need.

ID	❶	Task Name	Start	Finish	Duration	Assignee
1		**Warehouse Management System**	**Wed 9/21/05**	**Mon 3/27/06**	**134 days**	
2		Launch project	Wed 9/21/05	Wed 9/21/05	0 days	All
3		**Gather information requirements**	**Wed 9/21/05**	**Mon 10/24/05**	**24 days**	
4		**Conduct interviews**	**Wed 9/21/05**	**Wed 10/12/05**	**16 days**	
5		Begin interviews	Wed 9/21/05	Wed 9/21/05	0 days	
6		List interview sources	Wed 9/21/05	Thu 9/22/05	2 days	Jane
7		Schedule interviews	Fri 9/23/05	Fri 9/23/05	1 day	Fred
8		Develop interview questions	Wed 9/21/05	Fri 9/23/05	3 days	George
9		Perform and document interviews	Mon 9/26/05	Fri 10/7/05	10 days	Fred, Jane and George
10		Interpret interviews	Mon 10/10/05	Wed 10/12/05	3 days	All
11		Publish interview documentation	Wed 10/12/05	Wed 10/12/05	0 days	George
12		Observe work processes	Wed 9/21/05	Tue 9/27/05	5 days	All
13		Determine information domains	Thu 10/13/05	Mon 10/17/05	3 days	Mike
14		Develop information model	Tue 10/18/05	Mon 10/24/05	5 days	Mike
15		Finish gathering information requirements	Mon 10/24/05	Mon 10/24/05	0 days	
16		Develop specifications	Tue 10/25/05	Mon 11/21/05	20 days	Shirley
17		Write software	Tue 11/22/05	Mon 2/13/06	60 days	Shirley, Ron and George
18		Test software	Tue 2/14/06	Mon 3/27/06	30 days	Fred and Jane
19		Shut down project	Mon 3/27/06	Mon 3/27/06	0 days	

Figure 7/ *Task assignments*

A VERY USEFUL TRICK O' THE TRADE

Building a complete and accurate WBS is hard work, and a lot of it. Many novice project managers, overwhelmed by the size and magnitude of the task, stop a level or two short of a complete and manageable plan. The result is, with few exceptions, an out-of-control project.

Experienced project managers recognize the danger of too-high-level tasks, such as "Develop specifications" (Figure 7, Task 16, assigned to Shirley and estimated as a 20-day undertaking). They also recognize the danger of trying to do all the thinking themselves. And, if truth be told, they recognize the undesirability of taking on all of the hard work.

They recognize the superior alternative: Let Shirley figure it out.

When developing a WBS, get to a deep enough level that you can assign an owner to each chunk of work. Then let the owners figure out the rest. When they're finished, consolidate their efforts, establish interdependencies, and resolve any resource conflicts.

And, by the way, discuss any unrealistic estimates of task duration. You have two enemies here: optimism and padding. Optimism is what happens when project team members don't take into account all the ways obstacles can arise that will cause delays. Padding is what happens when a project team member figures it's easiest to succeed when the schedule provides ample time for project work, long walks on the beach, a few sets of tennis, and visits to the tanning booth. It's up to you to recognize optimism and padding, and to remove both from the plan.

Note the difference between delegating too-high-level tasks and delegating the planning. In the former case, neither you nor the project team member knows what has to get done for the task to finish. In the latter case you both do, and the team member, having had a great deal of say in formulating the plan, can commit to it.

You're still in for a lot of hard work, but nowhere near as much as if you'd had to handle all the planning yourself.

ONE MORE PLANNING TECHNIQUE

Projects encounter problems: Team members get sick. Hardware arrives late. Software needs patches from the vendor. A pipe breaks in the training room.

As project manager, you're responsible for completing all deliv-

STEP BY STEP
Projects finish on time, within budget and with all planned deliverables intact when:

1. *Everyone who has to perform project tasks knows what they should be working on at every stage of the project.*
2. *Everyone who has to perform project tasks receives task assignments that are short enough ... one to two weeks ... that they feel a sense of urgency getting them done.*
3. *The project manager is in a position to recognize when project tasks are late.*

To figure out the plan ...

1. *Outline it.*
2. *Let team members figure out the details of their assignments.*
3. *Finish groups of tasks with milestones - tasks of zero duration which mark the delivery of something tangible and clearly identifiable - so there's no question as to whether the project is on track or not.*
4. *And finally, build time to handle unforeseeable contingencies into the plan. They're unforeseeable, but that they'll happen is inevitable.*

erables on time and within the original budget. How do you handle these contingencies?

The answer is to scatter contingency tasks throughout the project plan, generally after major milestones. Give each contingency task between 10% and 25% of the time needed for the collection of tasks required to get to the milestone - less time if you're confident of what will be required to get to the milestone or if the collection of tasks is relatively short, more if you're mostly guessing or if the milestone is the result of a long, complex effort.

And if your business sponsor or some other stakeholder asks what the contingency tasks are for, be direct: "If I knew the answer to that, it wouldn't be called 'Contingency.' It would be called, 'Waiting until Shirley recovers from the flu.'"

THE LAUNCH

It might seem like a minor point, and in the greater scheme of things it is a minor point.

Still, take the time to formally launch your project. If you don't, there will be a morning when everyone wakes up and realizes, "Hey, the project has started!" Why make them wonder?

To formally launch the project, conduct a launch meeting. Even better, conduct two - one for everyone - the core team, extended team, sponsor and key stakeholders - the other for the just the core and extended team.

The first meeting is mostly symbolic, but does serve a practical purpose as well: It provides one more opportunity to help everyone work on the same project. After your introductions and a short cheerleading speech by the sponsor (don't underestimate its value - both team members and stakeholders will benefit from the sponsor emphasizing his/her personal commitment to the project, as well as its value to the company), use the rest of the hour to review the project's objective, goals and deliverables. Everyone should be familiar with them already. Do it anyway. Each step of the way, ask someone in the room … not always the same one … to explain the concept in different words, then ask everyone else if they think anything requires further clarification.

The project team will still have to go through the storming phase, but you might reduce its duration and intensity a bit.

Once the sponsors and stakeholders have left, everyone else

can get down to business. In the second hour, go around the room and have each participant review his or her role on the project. Distribute a contact list so everyone has everyone else's telephone number and e-mail address (and/or give them the URL where the list resides on the company intranet). Make the point that if anyone on the project needs to know something and someone else on the project team knows it, that's what telephones, e-mail and face-to-face visits are for.

LAUNCH - MEETING AGENDA

Item	Presenter/Facilitator	Time allotted
Welcome	Facilitator	5 minutes
Project business context	Executive sponsor	15 minutes
Project Statement of Objectives	Project manager; Group discussion	30 minutes
Project goals and deliverables	Project manager	15 minutes
Non-project-team attendees excused		
Roles and responsibilities; resource plan	Project manager; Group discussion	30 minutes
Initial task assignments	Project Manager & Team	30 minutes
Confirm status mtg. schedules	Project Manager & Team	5 minutes
Business tour(s)	Project Manager & Team	1 hr. per area

Table 3/ Sample Launch Meeting agenda

Next, hand out current copies of the project plan - the version that has names, tasks, start and finish dates on it, not the pretty Gantt Chart you handed out in the first meeting as part of the information packet you used to "dress the set." Go through every task assignment that's scheduled to start in the next week. Most of these will go to members of the core team, but many will depend on knowledge and involvement on the part of one or more members of the extended team. Make sure core team members are aware of this, and understand that involvement of the extended team isn't optional - it's part of the plan.

Especially if some project team members are relatively inexperienced, review the dependencies so everyone understands the impact of finishing an assignment late.

And finally, set the schedule for a weekly core-team status meeting, and a less-frequent (bi-weekly or monthly depending on the length of the project) full-team status meeting. What happens in the status meetings is covered in the next chapter.

Table 3 provides a sample agenda. Note that it finishes with a business tour or tours. Since the point is always about business improvement, asking the business participants to show the rest of the team their work area and how work flows through it is a good way to put some reality behind what the team is about to undertake.

The launch meeting finishes with you speaking these words: "That's it for the meeting. Time to get to work."

Speaking of which, that's it for this chapter. It's time to explain what "get to work" entails.

STEP BY STEP
Take the time to conduct a launch meeting:
1. *To make it official that the project has started.*
2. *To improve alignment of team members and stakeholders regarding the project's objective, goals, and deliverables.*
3. *To give team members their first work assignments so they know what they should be working on.*

MANAGING THE PROJECT

"Plan the work, work the plan."

A long, long time ago, Norman Vincent Peale coined this apho-
rism. When managing a project you'll get no better advice, but only
if you interpret it properly. If you don't, you're likely to buy a big
slab of granite and have your beautiful project plan etched into it.
If you do you'll ruin both your project and what would otherwise
become a perfectly good kitchen counter. Part of working the plan
is adjusting it as the situation changes.

The point of Peale's advice isn't to freeze the plan. It's to avoid
improvisation. Situations do arise, new discoveries invalidate
assumptions, risks turn into realities, and sometimes you or other
project team members find mistakes in the original plan. When that
happens, inexperienced project managers can become flustered [11].
They agree to any number of ready-fire-aim suggestions for resolv-
ing whatever it is.

They don't work the plan - they improvise.

But we're getting ahead of ourselves. The question is, once a
project launches and project team members are happily working
away at their assigned tasks, what's left for a project manager to do?
The answer is, not as much as before the project launches, but a lot
more than nothing at all. Project managers need to:

> Manage progress against the plan.

> Manage the emotional state of project team members.

[11] ManagementSpeak for "they panic."

> Facilitate the group dynamics of the project team.
> Manage the flow of great ideas that can change the project's scope and deliverables.
> Identify and develop contingency plans for potential risks.
> Identify and resolve issues as they arise.
> Communicate with all stakeholder groups.
> Keep the business sponsor informed and involved.

That's all.

MANAGING PROGRESS

Project managers often hear that they need to monitor the status of their project. This is one of those statement's that's just true enough to be misleading.

If monitoring status were enough, team members could send e-mails listing what they finished each week. That's monitoring status. By itself, it virtually ensures project chaos.

The title is "project manager," not "project monitor." Managing progress, instead of simply monitoring status, calls for face-to-face engagement … in a word, meetings.

WEEKLY STATUS MEETINGS

That meetings are wastes of time is a truism in business circles, especially among those whose primary responsibility is to perform real work (as opposed to managing real work). In the context of managing project progress, meetings are better described as overhead than waste, the difference being that overhead is often necessary where waste, by definition, is not.

Weekly status meetings are necessary overhead [12]. Despite the title, their purpose isn't to determine your project's status once each week, although that is one outcome. You conduct weekly status *meetings* for two reasons.

The first is to continue to build and maintain the alignment and trust that differentiates a team from a bunch of individuals with tasks to execute. By meeting they all hear the same information. They're able to clarify ambiguities - and when one team member asks for clarification and gets it, all the others hear the exchange as

---

[12] One might argue that since these remove an hour each week from the time available for useful work, that it's important for you to include that fact in your project planning. It would be a bad idea, for the same reason that removing the time needed for lunch and bathroom breaks would be a bad idea. The lost time represents 2.5% of a clock-watcher's workweek. If you take note of it, team members will start to use every interruption as a legitimate reason to extend their assignments.

well. They're in a position to recognize progress when it happens, offer each other support and assistance, and otherwise make sure they don't backslide from "performing" back to an earlier, less productive state.

The other reason to conduct weekly status meetings is to create peer pressure among project team members - something that doesn't happen with written status reports. Imagine you rely on the latter, and find out a task is going to be delayed. You have to take the initiative - you contact the team member and have to apply pressure yourself, making you the hard-case.

With a status meeting, team members who are late with tasks have to tell their peers, face-to-face, in real time. Nobody wants to tell their peers publicly that they messed up, so they'll do a lot to avoid having to do so. That's why it has to be a meeting - that, and so that when you ask the magic question, "What are you going to do to get back on track?" it becomes very difficult to answer, "Nothing - we'll just have to delay completion."

Which, by the way, demonstrates a subtlety: With good team members, the application of peer pressure never happens. Instead, team members put themselves under pressure to avoid disappointing their teammates.

AGENDA: WEEKLY STATUS MEETING

Pre-meeting schmoozing	5 min
Status of current tasks	20 min
Next week's plan	20 min
Risks and issues	5 min
News and information	10 min

Figure 8/ Sample agenda

Weekly status meetings are overhead, of course, so you want to keep them as brief and crisp as possible. Figure 8 provides a sample agenda. In order:

> *Pre-meeting schmoozing* is going to happen anyway. It's probably a good idea, too. Team members have to trust each other. Part of achieving this is to allow non-project-related chatter, joking, banter and all the other ways individuals turn each other into "we" instead of "they." (See "Team Maintenance" later on in this chapter for more on this subject.)

> *Status of current tasks* is where peer pressure happens. It's also where someone who's stuck can get help from someone else who was once stuck in a similar situation before[13]. And it's where you ask what the plan is for

[13] If that happens, it's an opportunity for you to ask the team member who's stuck why he or she didn't ask for help before the status meeting.

getting back on track. There will, by the way, be times when you have to accept project delays due to tasks being late, but these should be the exception. Since those responsible for tasks estimated the tasks during the planning phase, you're well within your rights to insist on longer days, and even weekend work on the part of the late team member to get the project back on schedule.

> ***Status of current tasks*** is also where you celebrate achievements. It's one thing for a project team member to state that this week's assignment - "Finish order entry module" - finished on schedule. It's another for you to say, "The rest of you might not be aware of just what Sylvia had to go through to get this module working properly. I know of at least five different undocumented interfaces she discovered while writing it. Great work, Sylvia."

> ***Status of current tasks*** covers one more subtopic - celebrating major milestones. Tasks finish every week, but with the completion of some tasks you get to announce recognizable progress outside the project team, too. "We've all been beating our brains out to get this phase finished on schedule. Monday, I get to tell the Steering Committee that we made it. Thanks - I love giving them good news. Great work all around to make this happen."

> ***Next week's plan:*** It's a good idea for everyone to know what everyone else will be working on. First, it's another way to reinforce that you're managing a project team rather than outsourcing tasks as piecework to separate individuals. And second, it's an opportunity for team members to ask to be consulted in decisions.

> ***Reminder:*** Gantt charts aren't very useful for project team members. They need a list of current tasks, sorted by team member and secondarily sorted by start date.

> ***Risks and issues:*** In the course of performing the work of the project, team members will discover risks you hadn't anticipated, and will face issues that require resolution. So will you. The weekly status meeting provides an opportunity for everyone to learn about them. Later in this chapter you'll find ideas on how to deal with risks and issues.

> ***News and information***: Sometimes you'll be made aware

of events or decisions elsewhere in the company that might affect the project. That information does you no good until you communicate it to the team. This is your chance.

One other recommendation: Task status is binary. A task is either complete or incomplete. Novice project managers often ask for an estimate of how close to completion a task is, accepting a percentage as an answer. It seems reasonable. But here's what happens:

A project team member who failed to complete a task on schedule, not wanting to admit to a serious problem (to him or herself just as much as to everyone else) will report that it's 80% done. A week later the task still isn't finished, but it can't be less finished than the week prior, so it's now 90% finished. It's akin to the Paradox of Zeno - the task gets closer and closer to its destination but never actually arrives.

MEETING NOTES

Yes, you have to publish meeting notes. No, you don't have to print them out, make copies, and distribute them. Instead, use technology. An especially useful technique in this day and age is to set up a project weblog on the company intranet for this purpose. You can publish the notes there; everyone who wants to can post comments and clarifications.

Meeting notes are important here for the same reason they're important for any meeting: You and everyone else can go back to remind yourselves what you agreed to, and why. They also provide a public record of progress and status.

MONTHLY STATUS MEETINGS

Once a month (more or less, depending on the project), invite the extended team to participate. It's pretty much the same meeting as the weekly status meetings, with two exceptions. First, it will require more time, because more people are in the room. And second, since the extended team won't have participated in the weekly status meetings, reserve time to bring its members up to date.

MANAGING EMOTIONS

Working on a project isn't the same as working on a day-to-day job. With day-to-day work, your efforts pay off immediately - you know what you've done and what it does for the organization. On a project you never know whether your efforts will pay off until after all deliverables are in the hands of the business. The result is an emotional roller coaster. As project manager you're as vulnerable to it as every other member of the project team. It will be up to you to help yourself through it, along with every other project team member.

As Figure 9 shows, the level of enthusiasm felt by typical project team members goes through a predictable trajectory.

> At the start is ***unenlightened optimism***: Team members are gung ho without thinking through what's in store. The goal is clear, the work hasn't started yet, and everyone is rarin'

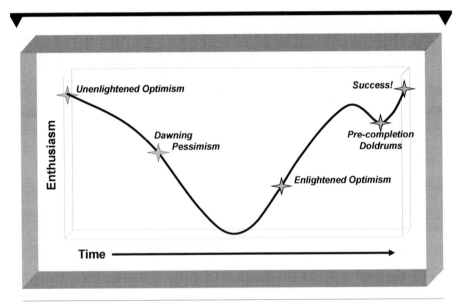

Figure 9 / *A project team's evolving emotional state*

to go. They don't know what they're in for - not in their gut where it matters - and they're sure the project is going to go smoothly, unlike the last one and the one before that.

> It isn't long, though, before the excitement of the launch fades. Since the end isn't yet in sight, it's easy to become demoralized. At this stage of the project, team members are subject to ***"dawning pessimism,"*** especially if obstacles start to appear. This is a dangerous time for a project team. As project manager, it's up to you to focus everyone on their day-to-day work. It's like running a long race (to use an overworked metaphor): For much of it, what matters most is putting one foot in front of the other. Thinking about the finish line is poisonous.

> After awhile, the team finds its groove and sees tangible progress. Its members have good reason to be optimistic. From the perspective of managing emotions, this stage - *"enlightened optimism"* - is the easiest period of the project.

> As with a long race, there comes a time in the life of every project when everyone is just plain tired and the finish line, while tantalizingly close, isn't close enough. Worse, the creative, challenging work is done. What's left is mostly a swarm of annoying details. It's the stage known as *"pre-completion doldrums."*

   Don't be afraid to give the team a break about now. Bring in pizza. Take everyone bowling. Get them outside if the climate allows it - some project teams go months without ever seeing sunlight.

> And finally, there's *success.* But that's the next chapter's subject.

Most formal project management training is about managing tasks, scope and risks. A lot of the day-to-day work is controlling your own emotional state and managing that of everyone else.

   Remember, and remind everyone else: If you put one foot in front of the other and continue heading in the right direction, eventually you'll reach your destination.

   Sure it's trite. It's also true.

FACILITATING GROUP DYNAMICS

One of the more aggravating aspects of working in teams is that teams don't spend all of their time and energy on The Work. Two other subjects occupy quite a bit of team time and energy: Personal needs and team maintenance.

PERSONAL NEEDS

Personal needs are issues that block individual team members, preventing them from moving forward and causing them to prevent the team from moving forward. Personal needs include such easy-to-solve issues as someone needing to know he was heard. They also include more difficult-to resolve challenges as engineering principles or affinities for specific technologies that are very hard for a professional to let go of.

   As project manager, it's up to you to recognize when a team

member is blocked by a personal issue, and to facilitate the team interaction to find a resolution.

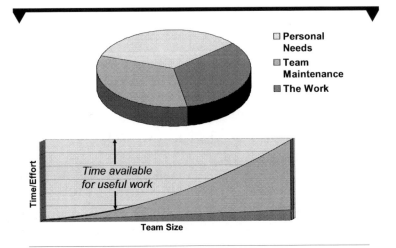

Figure 10/ Project team time budget

TEAM MAINTENANCE

Personal needs might be aggravating, but at least they're about the work. Team maintenance isn't even close. Team maintenance is banter, arguments about sports, gossip, and other time-wasters team members engage in for no other reason than to keep relationships on an even keel … and they don't even know that's what they're doing.

Project managers who don't understand this point try to eliminate these as time wasters. That's a bad idea: As explained in Chapter 2, for teams to perform well their members need to trust each other. Part of keeping that in place is banter, arguing about sports, and gossiping.

You can't prevent personal needs and team maintenance from distracting a project team, but you can keep them from getting out of hand. The most important tool at your disposal is minimizing the number of individuals who have to interact. The smaller the number, the less often you'll have a team member blocked by a personal need. More significantly, everyone will spend less time on team maintenance, which expands geometrically with team size[14]. In practical terms, this means minimizing the number of full-team

---

[14] If you're interested, it's because the number of pairs of team members who have to trust each other is determined by the formula $n*(n-1)/2$. Strictly speaking the number increases polynomially rather than exponentially.

meetings, maximizing the number of individual assignments, and doing your best to never assign any project task to more than three people.

There's one other technique you'll need to master in order to keep team dynamics healthy. Sometimes, two people just won't be able to work with each other. It happens. When it does there's no magic formula for fixing it. Do what you can to help them figure it out, and if they simply can't, rearrange tasks so they don't have to.

MANAGING SCOPE

There's never a shortage of great ideas. The shortage is of the time and energy needed to implement the great ideas. It's the Edison ratio: 1% inspiration, 99% perspiration.

Project managers rarely have to worry about whether enough great ideas will show up to help their project along. Quite the opposite, great ideas are a project manager's enemy: Every great idea that occurs to a project stakeholder can increase the project's scope, either by adding deliverables or by making the already-defined deliverables more complicated.

When a new great idea arrives, as project manager you have just a few alternatives, and just saying no isn't one of them. Neither is just saying yes, if you want to manage a successful project. What you can do is to work through the governance process defined for the project (covered in Chapter 1. In practical terms it means involving the project sponsor and Steering Committee in the decision, because otherwise they're sure to second-guess it) to arrive at one of these five possible decisions:

> Accept the idea, increasing the project's duration to accommodate it.

> Accept the idea, adding to the project team to accommodate it.

> Accept the idea, eliminating or redefining some of the original deliverables to make room for it.

> Put the idea in the next release, which means it goes into a different project and isn't your problem anymore.

> Reject the idea, as something whose costs don't justify the benefits.

There are two secrets to successful scope management: (1) Making it clear that nothing is free; and (2) "syndicating" the decision.

MANAGING RISKS

Optimists don't make good project managers. Optimists expect things to go right. Good project managers expect them to go wrong. More, they spend a lot of mental energy figuring out what's likely to go wrong and what they'll do when they do. In the lexicon of project management, they identify risks and develop contingency plans.

So should you. Involve your team to help you. Continue to do so throughout the project.

And ... and this is vitally important ... as you do, let your sponsor know about every risk you identify and get his or her approval - in advance - for your contingency plans. If appropriate, also include the Steering Committee if you have one so that when a risk turns into a reality you already have the authority to take action.

IDENTIFYING AND RESOLVING ISSUES

Things happen you either didn't or couldn't anticipate. Development environments have bugs. Capacity estimates turn out to be underestimates. Tasks take longer than expected. Process designs don't hold up to the close scrutiny of implementation.

And so on.

When things happen ... when issues arise ... successful project managers have to obey four rules or they're doomed to failure. These rules are:

1. You have to build enough trust with the project team that they tell you about them.
2. You have to be good enough at listening, and at organizational listening, to avoid mistaking testimony for fact. If you hear about a problem your first step is usually to investigate further, not to act.
3. You have to be brutally honest with yourself - honest enough to not try to persuade yourself the issue will resolve itself.
4. If the issue exceeds your authority to resolve, you have to be brutally honest with the project sponsor - honest enough to persuade the project sponsor the issue won't resolve itself.

If you obey these four rules, and follow the defined governance process, you won't get burned by unresolved issues.

COMMUNICATE

Projects have stakeholders - everyone who cares or is concerned about how the project turns out. As time permits, keep them apprised of your progress. If time doesn't permit, take time to keep them apprised anyway, even if it's nothing more than some quick e-mail messages to a distribution list.

Projects are about change. Change can make people nervous, especially if they know it will affect them and aren't sure how. Do what you can to reassure them, and if you can't do that, do what you can to reduce their uncertainty. If you don't, they'll reduce it themselves, by listening to and feeding the rumor mill. You're better off giving them accurate information than allowing that to happen.

Trick o' the trade: Show what you plan to communicate to the project team before you send it out to get their reaction. You get two benefits. First, you'll send out a better communication. Second, the project team will know you're bragging about them to the rest of the company.

Trick o' the trade #2: Many ... make that most projects have a political impact. This means most projects will have detractors in the corporation - not because the detractors are bad people, but because they disagree with the decision to go forward.

Keep your detractors informed too. And, anticipate what they're likely to be saying, and whom they'll be saying it too. Do your best to defuse whatever issues you think they're likely to raise.

KEEP YOUR BUSINESS SPONSOR INFORMED

Your business sponsor is your partner. You need to keep it that way. The way to do so is to keep your sponsor informed and involved. To do that, meet weekly at a scheduled time and a fixed agenda. Figure 11 provides a sample.

Without information and involvement you can easily turn your business sponsor from a partner and collabora-

AGENDA: WEEKLY STATUS MEETING	
Pre-meeting schmoozing	10 min
Project status	20 min
New risks and issues	20 min
Sponsor issues	10 min

Figure 11/ *Sample agenda*

tor into a project critic. You'll recall from Chapter 1 that without a project sponsor the chances of completing a project successfully are much lower, and the chance of achieving the point of it all ... business change ... is just about nil. If, by failing to inform and involve the business sponsor, you turn the sponsor into a critic, you'll have killed your own project.

Sometimes it turns out that your business sponsor isn't your partner - that the "sponsor" is sponsor in name only. When this happens it's up to you to turn the "sponsor" into your partner. The tools at your disposal are constant communication and constant attempts at involvement (primarily by escalating issues and decisions). In extreme circumstances you might find yourself having to "offer" to kill the project (by saying, "If you don't want this to happen, why are we doing it?"), or having to list lack of sponsor commitment as a project risk, triggering escalation to the steering committee.

Of all the situations a project manager faces, having a sponsor in name only is the most challenging. Dealing with it effectively requires a delicate combination of courage and diplomacy. Failing to deal with it effectively, though, can result in career disaster.

STEP BY STEP
On a regular basis:
1. *Manage progress against the plan.*
2. *Manage the emotional state of project team members.*
3. *Facilitate the group dynamics of the project team.*
4. *Manage the flow of great ideas that can change the project's scope and deliverables.*
5. *Identify and develop contingency plans for potential risks.*
6. *Identify and resolve issues as they arise.*
7. *Communicate with all stakeholder groups.*
8. *Keep the business sponsor informed and involved.*

DECLARING VICTORY

All good things must come to an end. Among them, by definition, are good projects. Bad projects, in contrast, drift on for a seeming eternity, unending, unproductive, and somehow unkillable.

You, of course, are managing a good project. It's going to end, and you're going to end it - cleanly and professionally.

Projects drift on without end for a variety of reasons. Many do so because they've violated one or more of the principles presented in the previous chapters: They don't end because they aren't finished and never will be. Perhaps the scope has crept and continues to creep. Maybe consensus regarding definition of deliverables is lacking. A change in sponsorship might have dragged the project back to the starting gate.

But some projects fail to finish because their project managers don't know how to declare victory so that everyone can return to their farms and villages (okay, their offices and cubicles). Sometimes, finishing a project is as simple as knowing how and when to stop.

Knowing how to stop begins with individual tasks. There's a disease among engineers that's the result of their desire for perfection. Faced with a deliverable they can always find another way to tweak it, improve it, fix one more thing or add one more feature that will make it just a bit cooler and more admirable. *This tendency has led to the adage that there comes a time in the life of every project when you have to shoot the engineers and put the product into production.*

On a task by task basis, know how to inform reluctant project team members that they've achieved the exalted state of Good Enough and it's time to move on to the next task.

Business sponsors and project participants have a related disorder: The instinctive desire to discover unimportant aesthetic flaws. These can drag a project on for a lifetime for the simple reason that no two people will completely agree about aesthetics, so satisfying one critic will create another.

Project managers can prevent the worst of the aesthetics adjustment problem by the technique, described in Chapter 3, of creating an extended team. This turns the most likely critics into collaborators. It also helps ensure consensus around aesthetic issues during the course of the project - "end-user acceptance testing" becomes a daily collaboration instead of an end-of-project annoyance.

The most pernicious reason for failure to stop was described years ago by Gerry Friesen in an article in *Teleconnect* magazine. He called it the 98% solution. According to Friesen, any employee on any day can take any assignment and carry it to 98% of completion. Most stop there, though, because it isn't until they finish the final 2% that they find out whether they were right or wrong - whether whatever-it-was you asked them to do will, in fact, work in practice.

Project teams have the exact same tendency. It's up to you to get the team past it. How you do it depends on the exact circumstances, but most often the best way is akin to the technique for getting horses out of a burning barn. You have to put the blinders on.

In the case of a project team, this means little more than continuing what you did when the team entered the "Dawning Pessimism" phase of the project. You focus each team member on the immediate task, doing your best to avoid drawing attention to the approaching finish line.

They will, of course, notice eventually but that's okay: They'll notice when they're working on the final task or two, and by then they'll be trapped into wrapping things up.

(Sometimes you'll face the opposite problem: Members of the project team will be slated to join another project that's ramping up to launch, and will want to finish their project tasks as expeditiously as possible. This isn't entirely a bad thing either - it helps get everyone through the pre-completion doldrums. The risk, of course, is that they'll do a quick-and-dirty job of the tasks that stand between them and their new assignment.)

IT IS PART OF THE PLAN, ISN'T IT?

One of the basic mistakes made in many software project plans is that they don't include transition tasks - the activities that start when the software has been installed. Other types of projects have similar issues - for example, when constructing or remodeling a building, some plans finish when the building is ready for occupancy instead of when it is occupied.

Take a fresh look at your project plan. Assuming you're managing a software project, if it doesn't include the actions needed to put its deliverables into productive use, add them now. Typically, these start with training in the software and how to perform each job in the business using the software. They might include a pilot roll-out, and a phased introduction into different areas of the business (always preferred when feasible)[15].

Unless, that is, these tasks are formally out of scope for one reason or another (see Chapter 2) - either because they are part of a different, linked project, or because the are, for some reason, unnecessary. If that's the case, make sure your plan includes the tasks necessary to turn the software over to the next project team.

When geographically possible, turn the project team into floorwalkers for the first week or two of use, to get end-users over the worst of the transition. Doing so leads to three very desirable results:

> End-users get immediate face-to-face assistance with problems.
> The project team gets immediate exposure to bugs and ease-of-use problems.
> The project team also gets to see the results of their efforts being put to productive use. That's a very cool experience - nothing else you can do will provide such a strong sense of accomplishment.

Whatever your project and whatever the specifics, if it finishes with you delivering the software, installing it, training the users and stopping, your project will probably never finish. That's because the project sponsor won't let you finish it - and shouldn't[16].

[15] If you decide to do this now, handle the situation as a change in scope, the same way you'd handle any other change in scope. Refer back to Chapter 6 for the specifics. And remember to include these tasks when developing the plan in your next project.

[16] Another common missing piece: If the project is to replace an existing piece of software, the project plan has to include the tasks necessary to unplug the old software. It seems obvious, but fails to happen far too often.

ENGAGE THE PROJECT SPONSOR

As completion approaches, one very important step to take is to prime the sponsor for completion. About a month before the final task is scheduled to complete, confirm with the sponsor that when this task has finished, he/she will consider the project to be finished and successful. If the answer is no, or ambiguous, ask what else will be required.

POST-PROJECT REVIEWS
Well-run companies take care to find out if projects deliver the planned benefits. While important, these aren't and shouldn't be the responsibility of the project manager, for two very important reasons:

> *The benefits don't appear immediately following project completion, so the review shouldn't take place until six months later. By then, you'll be fully occupied with your next project.*

> *The project manager wasn't responsible for determining the planned business benefits. As project manager, you're responsible for providing all deliverables on time, on schedule, and within budget. The business sponsor is responsible for delivering the benefits.*

If making the business changes necessary to achieve the planned benefits was within the project scope (and, therefore, included in the project plan) then you should be part of the post-project review when it happens.

But since sustaining the change is a process that begins when the project ends, you should be careful. As is true of so many facets of project management, if someone doesn't like something that has to do with the project, you're first in line when the blamestorming starts.

Some sponsors will be uncomfortable committing to an answer, insisting on a wait-and-see approach. It's understandable from an emotional perspective - making the commitment has a finality to it that can create serious uncertainty. You'll have to help the sponsor through this, because otherwise the project team will be left in limbo for an indefinite period of time.

Just keep asking: Here are the deliverables we agreed to. Here is our definition of success. Has anything changed? If not, let's stick to the plan we started with.

SCHEDULE A COMPLETION MEETING

The project starts with a launch meeting. It should finish with a completion meeting. It isn't that meetings have any particular magic to them. It's that doing so makes completion clean. Before the completion meeting the project was still going on. After it, the project is entirely over - no residual tasks, no niggling details, nothing. It's done. Time to move on to the next project.

The completion meeting doesn't have to be formal. Mostly, it's an opportunity for you, the project sponsor, and possibly another high-profile executive to thank the project team for its efforts. It's basic good manners and costs nobody anything worth counting.

Even the most cynical project team members will appreciate the gesture, and its absence would be noticed by even the least cynical.

SCHEDULE A CELEBRATION

Celebrate victories. One reason is that they're worth celebrating. Another - less heartwarming but certainly worth paying attention to - is that celebrating the successful completion of a project has become something of a tradition, which means it's an entitlement. It doesn't have to be lavish, but it does have to happen.

Especially with a small project, the completion meeting and celebration can be the same event. Extend it over the lunch hour, and either bring in lunch or take everyone out.

Also consider giving team members a wee giftie as a token of appreciation and a remembrance of the project - a tee shirt, coffee mug or other item that will trigger fond memories of a good project that finished well.

SCHEDULE A PROJECT DEBRIEFING MEETING

This is optional, but if you're planning to manage more projects it's a good idea. The debriefing meeting should include the core and extended team members, the project sponsor, and other stakeholders. The agenda has three items:

> What went well on the project, so everyone knows to do it again in the next one.
> What went poorly, so everyone knows not to do it on the next one.
> What else was learned that can be applied to future projects.

This is a tough conversation to get started in some business cultures that aren't accustomed to frank discussions of issues. If you set the right tone during the project itself, though, candor should be second-nature to everyone in the room.

ARCHIVE KEY PROJECT DOCUMENTS

You don't have to keep everything. You should keep enough to document everything that happened, every decision ... everything that might be called into question once memories have faded. It's unfortunate, but self-protection sometimes becomes a necessity for project managers, and you're better off prepared than hoping you won't need the documentation.

Some companies have formal procedures for archiving project documents. If yours is one of them, keep a private copy as well. Just in case.

FIGURE OUT HOW TO SPEND YOUR TIME

Your whole routine is built around managing the project, and now the project is over. Chances are good you'll be at loose ends for awhile, trying to figure out what you should be doing. That's okay - you need a break anyway.

ACKNOWLEDGE TO YOURSELF THAT IT'S OVER

Managing a project and writing a book have quite a bit in common. At the beginning, the effort can look impossibly large. You get through it by establishing a schedule and a routine. You have to know when you're done.

And when you're done you have to know when to stop.

▼ ▼

STEP BY STEP

Recognize and address the common causes of project "drift":

1. *The 98% solution - fear of finding out whether it will actually work.*
2. *Not including the tasks required to put the project's deliverables to productive use.*
3. *Not knowing how to say, "stop - we're done now."*

To make sure the project finishes and shuts down ...

1. *Engage the project sponsor.*
2. *Schedule a completion meeting.*
3. *Schedule a celebration.*
4. *Schedule a post-project debriefing.*

When it is over ...

1. *Archive key project documents.*
2. *Figure out how to spend your time.*
3. *Acknowledge to yourself that it's over.*

Made in the USA